AF449062

# YOU'LL KNOW IT WHEN YOU SEE IT! UNIQUELY GEEKY THINGS

## GEOGRAPHY BOOKS FOR KIDS CHILDREN'S GEOGRAPHY & CULTURE BOOKS

In this book, we're going to talk about geeky inventions to .use when traveling the world. So, let's get right to it!

There are so many new geeky gadgets and inventions that come out every year. Some of these inventions are very helpful or fun if you're traveling to different countries around the world. They can make you more comfortable on your travels, help you keep connected to friends and family, and even sanitize your drinking water.

KID HAVING FUN IN SWIMMING POOL.

# SPECTACLES

Are you a fan of Snapchat? Then, you may want these special sunglasses. By using these sunglasses you can protect your eyes from the sun and at the same time you can take 10-second video clips and sync them to your Snapchat account.

While you're exploring an ancient monastery or basking at the beach or dancing in a festival, you can take video clips of whatever you're seeing, and send them to your smartphone, without using your hands! The case for the glasses has a battery charger as well as a USB cable.

# LUGGAGE SCOOTER

Would you like to zoom around the airport with your luggage? Then, you may want to buy a luggage scooter that has a built-in travel bag. You can pack your bag and then when you're in the airport you can use it like a scooter.

It's fun to ride and it gets you to your terminal in less than half the time as walking with a rolling luggage bag. Some of these scooters even have built-in Bluetooth so you can listen to music while you're rushing to catch your plane.

KID SUNBATHING ON COLORFUL BEACH MAT

# SANDLESS BEACH MAT

Do you like to bask on the beach but don't like the sand? Then, you may want to buy a sandless beach mat. These mats were originally designed for the military to use. When military helicopters landed in sandy areas, the dust and sand kicked up causing a safety hazard.

The same type of mat has been designed for beach lovers so they can relax on the beach without getting sand between their toes. The mat has a unique two-layer mesh design that just allows sand to fall through instead of sticking.

# SIGMO

Would you like people to understand what you're saying no matter what country you're in? Then, you may want to buy a Sigmo. This very tiny hand-held device can take what you say and translate it into the language of the country you're visiting. Suppose you're a French traveler and you're visiting Germany. You're lost and need to ask directions.

You can talk into the device in French and it will translate what you've said to the person you're speaking to in German. Then, when the person talks back to you in German, it will translate what he or she has said into French. Sigmo can be used with earphones as well as speakers so you can use it while you're making phone calls. It translates 25 different languages.

KID WEARING COOLING T-SHIRT

# THE COOLING T-SHIRT

Are you planning to make a trip to the desert? Then, you may want to buy a special t-shirt that's designed to cool you off. The fabric in this shirt contains xylitol, which is actually a replacement for sugar, but also has cooling properties. It gives you a sensation of cooling on the surface of your skin. It also helps you stay protected from the harmful UV rays of the sun.

# THE PORTABLE WATER STERILIZER

Are you going to a country that has unsanitary water? Then, you may want to buy a handheld water purifier. You place the device in water and within a minute and a half it can purify an entire liter of water. It kills almost all the germs in the water, up to 99.9%, so that you won't get sick on your travels. It works by using ultraviolet light.

WOMAN TAKING WATER FROM STREAM

GIRL USING THE TRAY

# THE AIR HOOK

Have you ever been very uncomfortable in your airplane seat because of the pull-down tray? Then, you may want to buy an air hook. This is a new device that hooks on to the closed tray. Because you don't have to open the pull-down tray, you'll have more space to spread out and be comfortable in your seat. It holds a plastic cup firmly so that you can have something to drink while you're relaxing.

It also holds your smartphone or tablet at eye level so that you can surf the web while you're in the air. It has an adjustable bungee so you can easily reposition your phone or tablet if the passenger in front of you is one of those people who are always bouncing around.

# THE SMART SUITCASE

Would you like a suitcase that would send you an alert if it's separated from you? Then, you may want a Bluesmart suitcase. You can use your smartphone to lock it or unlock it. It can weigh itself and it can be tracked no matter where you are in the world because it has a built-in global positioning system, GPS for short.

Time in a trip: 23 days 18 hours 43 minutes
LOCK BAG
UNLOCK BAG
DISTANCE 10 m
SMART suit
W

se

It syncs up with your itinerary so it give you assistance on your world travels. It can even charge all your hand-held devices or a laptop computer.

COUPLE TAKING A SELFIE

# THE POSTAGRAM

Do you want to send a postcard about your travels but don't have a stamp or a printer handy? Then, you will want to send a postagram. You can access the postagram app on your smartphone. Then, you can pick any photo you've taken on your travels and send a customized message in one of 15 different languages.

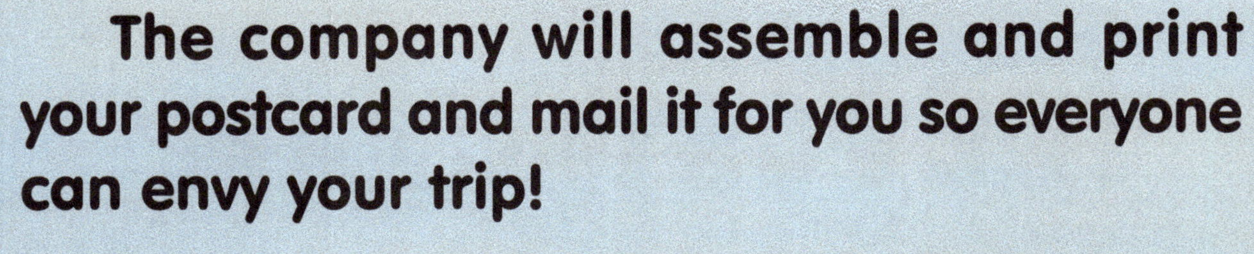

The company will assemble and print
your postcard and mail it for you so everyone
can envy your trip!

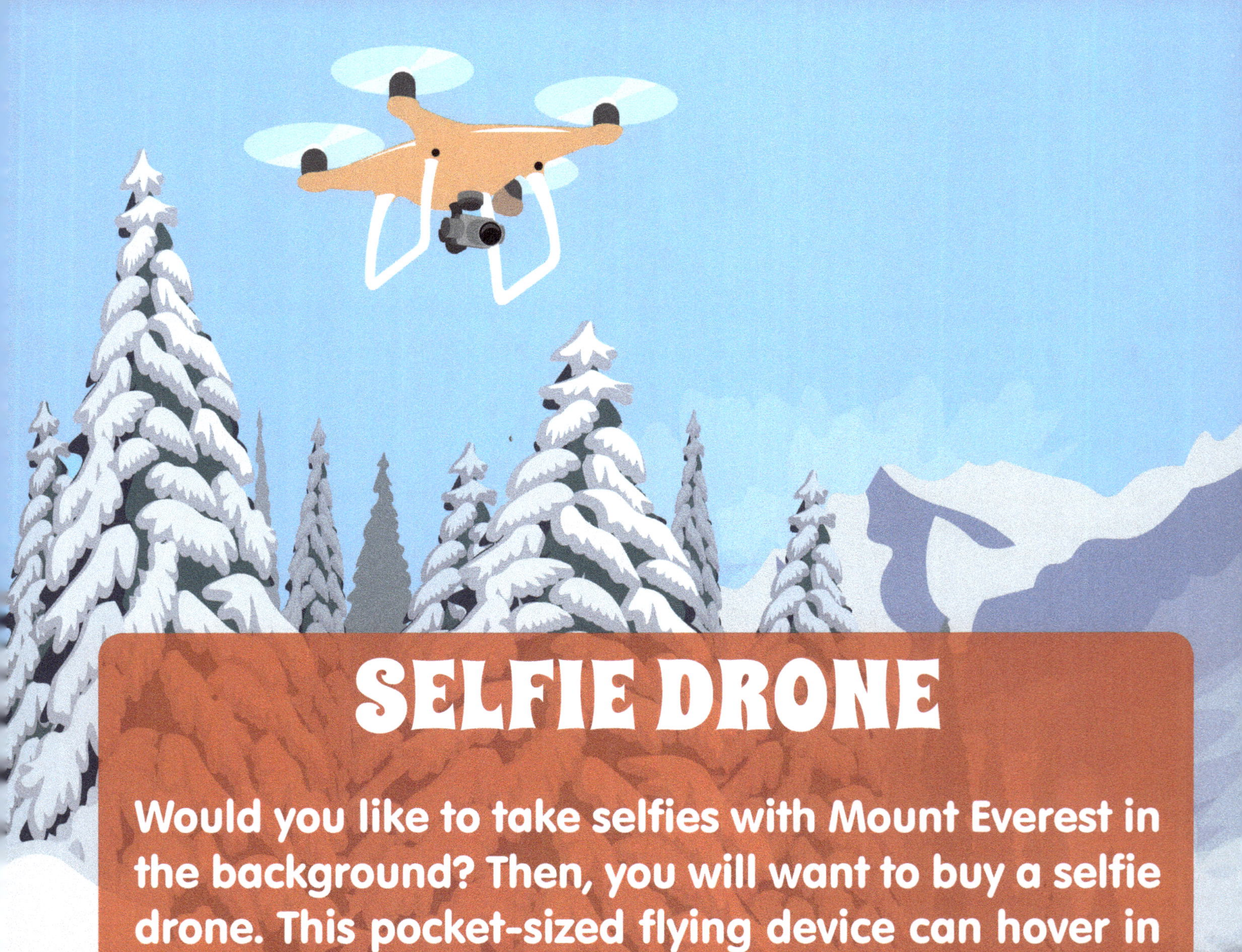

# SELFIE DRONE

Would you like to take selfies with Mount Everest in the background? Then, you will want to buy a selfie drone. This pocket-sized flying device can hover in the air about 20 meters away as you snap selfies with you, your friends, and the tallest mountain in the world. It has a 5-megapixel camera and can fly for a full 3 minutes.

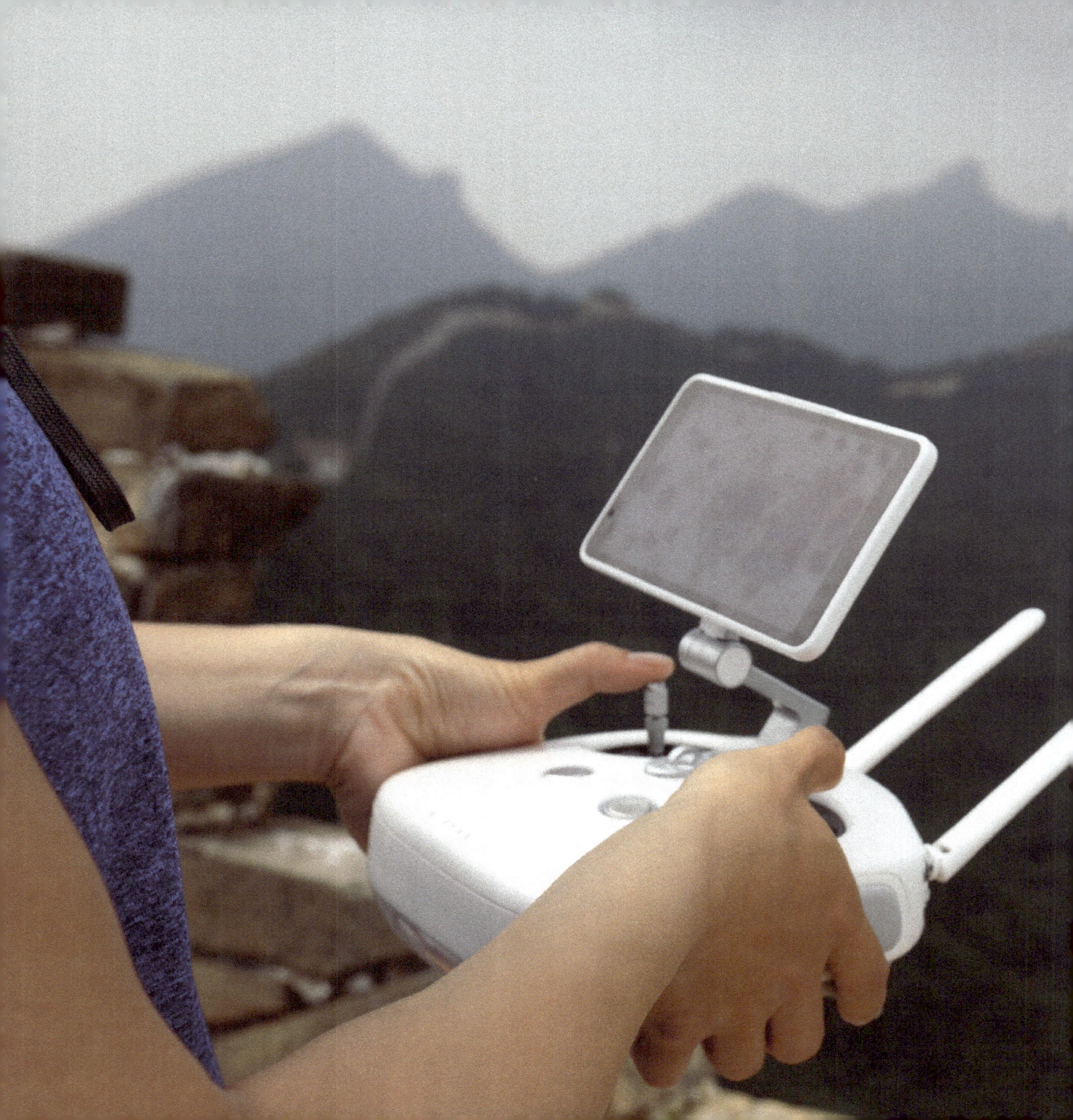

To control the drone, you use your smartphone. Your images as well as video clips are stored on a MicroSD card that has 4 gigabytes of space. You can also sync your images to a photo library in the cloud or share it with your friends and family back home by using an app.

PILE OF LAUNDRY

# POCKET-SIZED WASHING MACHINE

Are you in the outback but really need to wash your clothes? Then, you will want to use a Scrubba Washing Bag. This pocket-sized bag helps you do your laundry anywhere in the world that has a clean water source. It has a washboard that's flexible.

You only need about 4 liters of water and a small amount of liquid soap to use it and you can get your clothes clean in just a few minutes.

LAUNDRY DETERGENT

LADIES PACKED SUITCASE

# TIDY-SNAP

Do you dislike packing up your clothes when it's time to travel somewhere else? Then, you need Tidy-Snap. It's a system that helps you roll your clothes. There are three pieces that make it work. There's a board that helps you fold the clothes, plastic rods to roll the clothes up, and a snapping strip that keeps each item of your clothing rolled in place.

It helps you pack quickly and neatly. When you get home you can use it to keep your dresser drawers neat too.

ROLLED-UP SHIRTS

TOURIST USING NAVIGATION APP ON A MOBILE PHONE.

# THE TREASURE TAG

Are you afraid that you'll leave something important in a foreign country and never see it again? Then, you may want to buy some treasure tags. These tags can be attached to anything important like your keys or your bag. They are specifically designed to help you find something that you've left behind or lost. They work using an app on your smartphone.

# THE LUGGAGE TRACKER

Are you and your luggage always getting separated? Then, you may want to get a luggage tracker. There are several different brands on the market. You place a tracking device in your suitcase and sync it to an app on your smartphone. It sends you a text message like "you've got underwear" when the luggage arrives at the proper location.

It can even sense an airplane's movement so that it switches into a special airplane mode while your luggage is up in the air. Once the plane has landed, it uses the regional phone network to send a message to you.

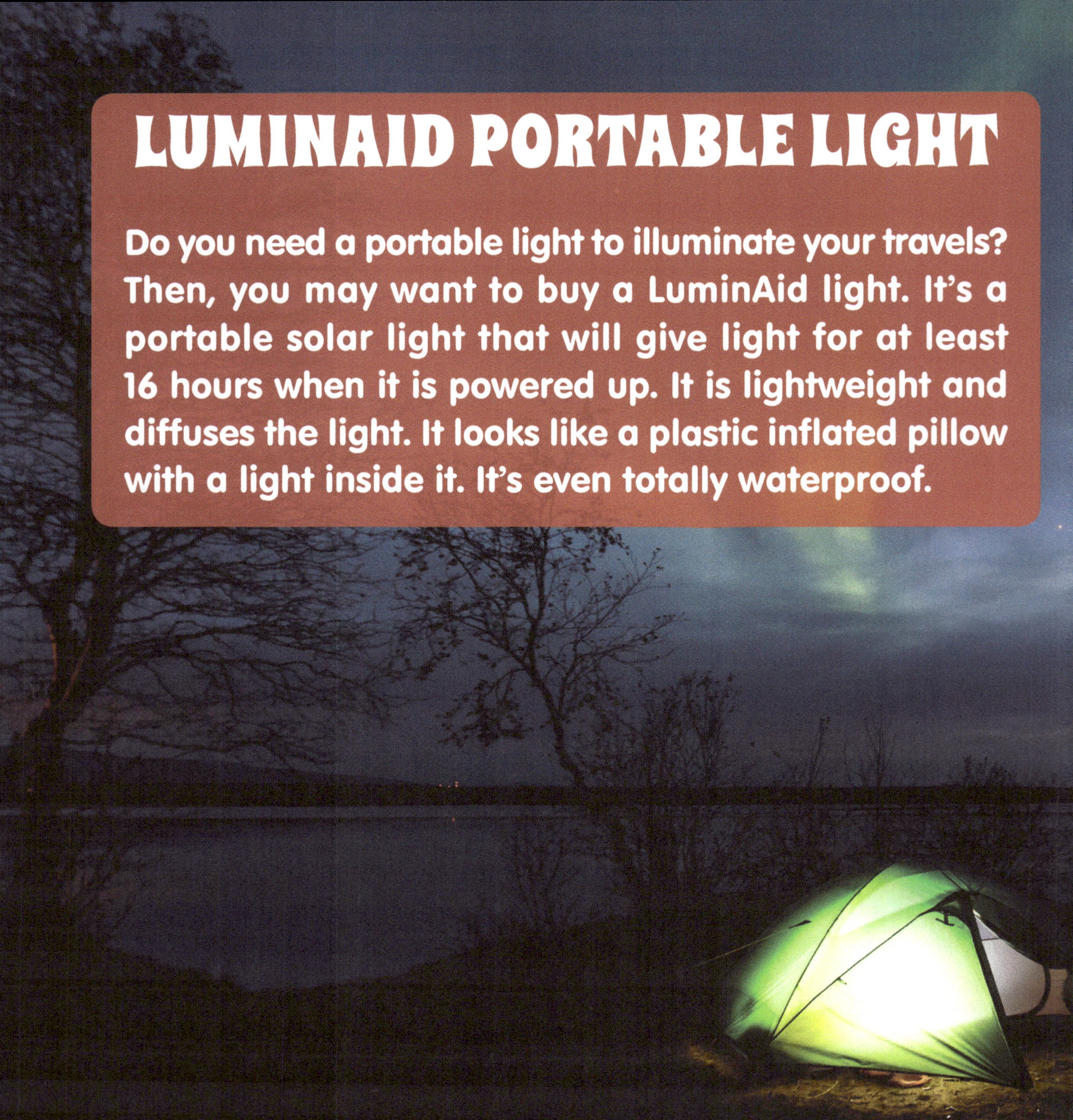

# LUMINAID PORTABLE LIGHT

Do you need a portable light to illuminate your travels? Then, you may want to buy a LuminAid light. It's a portable solar light that will give light for at least 16 hours when it is powered up. It is lightweight and diffuses the light. It looks like a plastic inflated pillow with a light inside it. It's even totally waterproof.

CAMPING USING PORTABLE SOLAR LIGHT

YOUNG INVENTORS

# So Many Gadgets!

New high-tech, geeky inventions and gadgets are being produced every year. These fun and useful items help you enjoy your travels and stay safe. Some of them, like the water sanitizer, might even save your life.

Awesome! Now that you've read about geeky inventions, you may want to read more information about hobby drones in the Baby Professor book How Do Drones Work? Technology Book for Kids.

Visit
BABY PROFESSOR
EDUCATION KIDS
www.BabyProfessorBooks.com
to download Free Baby Professor eBooks
and view our catalog of new and exciting
Children's Books